Shaped by God

thinking & feeling
in tune with the Psalms

JOHN PIPER

Contents

PSALM 1

Blessed is the man
who walks not in the counsel of the wicked,
nor stands in the way of sinners,
nor sits in the seat of scoffers;
but his delight is in the law of the LORD,
and on his law he meditates day and night.

He is like a tree
planted by streams of water
that yields its fruit in its season,
and its leaf does not wither.
In all that he does, he prospers.
The wicked are not so,
but are like chaff that the wind drives away.

Therefore the wicked will not stand in the judgment,
nor sinners in the congregation of the righteous;
for the LORD knows the way of the righteous,
but the way of the wicked will perish.

1
Songs That Shape the Heart and Mind

PSALM 1

As we examine how we can learn to think and feel in tune with the Psalms, and come to be shaped by God, there are three things we should know about the Psalms: they are instructive, they are poems, and they are from God.

Psalms Are Instructive

First, the Psalms are meant to be instructive about God and human nature and life. When we read the Psalms, we are meant to learn things about God, and about human nature, and about how life is to be lived. Some poetry makes no claim to instruct the mind, but the Psalms do.

One of the pointers to this instruction (among many pointers, including the doctrinal use made of the Psalms in the New Testament) is that Psalm 1 introduces the whole book of Psalms. The book begins, in a sense, in Psalm 1:2, "His delight is in the law of the Lord, and on his law he meditates day and night." The word for law is *torah*, and the general meaning for *torah* is instruction. In other words, the Psalms cover the whole range of God's instruction, not just legal ordinances. The entire book of Psalms is introduced by a call to meditate on God's instruction.

Furthermore, consider the way the book of Psalms is structured. It is divided into five books that begin with Psalms 1, 42, 73, 90, and 107. Each collection of psalms ends with a kind of special doxology that marks the end of each book. From the earliest times, these five divisions have been seen as a conscious effort to make the Psalms parallel to the five books of Moses (Genesis, Exodus, Leviticus, Numbers, and Deuteronomy), which are usually called the "law" books.[1]

So when Psalm 1 introduces all five books in the Psalter by saying that the righteous person meditates on the law of the Lord day and night, it probably means that these five books of Psalms, not just the five books of Moses, are the law of the Lord—the instruction of the Lord— that we should meditate on day and night. Therefore, for this reason and others, the Psalms are meant to be instructive about God and human nature and life.

Psalms Are Poems

The second thing we should know about the Psalms is that they are poems. That's what *psalm* means. They are meant to be read or sung as poetry or songs. The point of this observation is that poetry or singing is intended to stir up and carry the affections of the heart. So the Psalms are not just about thinking, but also feeling.

If you read the Psalms only for doctrine, you're not

reading them for what they are. They are psalms, songs, poetry. They're musical, and the reason that human beings express truth with music and poetry is to awaken and express emotions that fit the truth.

One of the reasons the Psalms are deeply loved by so many Christians is that they give expression to an amazing array of emotions, including:

Loneliness: "I am lonely and afflicted" (Psalm 25:16).

Love: "I love you, O Lord, my strength" (Psalm 18:1).

Awe: "Let all the inhabitants of the world stand in awe of him!" (Psalm 33:8).

Sorrow: "My life is spent with sorrow" (Psalm 31:10).

Regret: "I am sorry for my sin" (Psalm 38:18).

Contrition: "A broken and contrite heart, O God, you will not despise" (Psalm 51:17).

Discouragement and turmoil: "Why are you cast down, O my soul, and why are you in turmoil within me?" (Psalm 42:5).

Shame: "Shame has covered my face" (Psalm 44:15).

Exultation: "In your salvation how greatly he exults!" (Psalm 21:1).

Marveling: "This is the Lord's doing; it is marvelous in our eyes" (Psalm 118:23).

Delight: "His delight is in the law of the Lord" (Psalm 1:2).

Joy: "You have put more joy in my heart than they have when their grain and wine abound" (Psalm 4:7).

Gladness: "I will be glad and exult in you" (Psalm 9:2).

Fear: "Serve the LORD with fear" (Psalm 2:11).

Anger: "Be angry, and do not sin" (Psalm 4:4).

Peace: "In peace I will both lie down and sleep" (Psalm 4:8).

Grief: "My eye wastes away because of grief" (Psalm 6:7).

Desire: "O LORD, you hear the desire of the afflicted" (Psalm 10:17).

Hope: "Let your steadfast love, O LORD, be upon us, even as we hope in you" (Psalm 33:22).

Brokenheartedness: "The LORD is near to the brokenhearted and saves the crushed in spirit" (Psalm 34:18).

Gratitude: "I will thank you in the great congregation" (Psalm 35:18).

Zeal: "Zeal for your house has consumed me" (Psalm 69:9).

Pain: "I am afflicted and in pain" (Psalm 69:29).

Confidence: "Though war arise against me, yet I will be confident" (Psalm 27:3).

More explicitly than all the other books in the Bible, the Psalms are designed to awaken and shape our emotions as they provide instruction. When you read and sing the

Psalms the way they are intended to be read and sung, your emotions and your mind are shaped by their words.

Psalms Are from God

One last important point to know about the Psalms, by way of introduction, is that they are inspired by God. They are not merely the words of man but also the words of God. That means that God guided what was written and arranged them such that the Psalms teach the truth and, when properly understood, give the right direction to the emotions.

One of the reasons that we believe that the Psalms are divinely inspired and trustworthy is that Jesus does. In Mark 12:36, Jesus quotes Psalm 110:1, saying, "David himself, in [or by] the Holy Spirit, declared, 'The Lord said to my Lord, "Sit at my right hand, until I put your enemies under your feet."'" Jesus believes that David spoke *by the Holy Spirit* (see Acts 4:25; 2 Peter 1:21). In John 10:35, he quotes Psalm 82:6 and says, "Scripture cannot be broken." And in John 13:18 he quotes Psalm 41:9 and says, "The Scripture will be fulfilled." Jesus believes in the reliability of the Psalms.

Therefore, the Psalms are both man's words and God's words. What man expresses through each poem, God also expresses for his purposes. When we read and sing the Psalms, our minds and hearts—our thinking and feeling—are being shaped by God.

Shaping Power of the Psalms

The miracle of the new birth shows us that the Holy Spirit raises the spiritually dead by giving them new minds and hearts that together believe the gospel, love God, and want to be conformed to Christ. And yet, born-again people are not perfected. They are truly new, truly alive, truly spiritual, but in many ways unformed and immature—just like newborns in our families.

So the question for the early Christians—and for us—is this: How does the new mind and the new heart, full of imperfect thinking and feeling, pursue the fullness of right-thinking and the fullness of holy affections?

One of the main answers of early church believers was to immerse themselves in the Psalms. Psalms is the most often-quoted Old Testament book in the New Testament. It was the songbook, poetry book, and meditation book of the church. Alongside the teachings of Jesus and the apostles, Psalms was the book that shaped the thinking and feeling of the first disciples more than any other.

It is this shaping power of the Psalms that gets at my aim in this short book. My hope is to simply jump-start, or deepen, that kind of Psalms legacy in your life. I pray for God-centered, Christ-exalting, Psalms-saturated thinking and feeling—because I believe that this kind of thinking and feeling will bear fruit in the kind of living that cares for people and magnifies Christ.

Three Questions on Psalm 1

As we take a closer look at Psalm 1, we will see both of our themes—thinking and feeling. Let's consider three observations that come from three questions.

1. Why Does the Psalmist Begin the Way He Does?

Why does the psalmist begin, "Blessed is the man who walks not in the counsel of the wicked, nor stands in the way of sinners, nor sits in the seat of scoffers" (v.1)? Why not just say, "Don't be wicked, don't sin, and don't scoff"? Why draw attention to the wicked, the sinner, and the scoffer? Why focus on where we look for influence? Why repeat the warnings: "Don't be influenced by the wicked. Don't be influenced by the sinner. Don't be influenced by the scoffer"?

The reason is that the contrast he wants to draw is not wickedness versus righteousness, but influence from one place versus influence from another. The contrast is about being shaped in one way versus being shaped in another. Will we be shaped in our thinking and feeling by the wicked, the sinner, and the scoffer? Or will we be shaped by the instruction of the Lord?

So the psalmist sets up verse 1 the way he does to prepare for the contrast in verse 2. Don't give your attention to the world (the wicked, the sinner, the scoffer) so that you start to delight in their ways. Rather, speaking of the blessed man in verse 2, "his delight is in the law of the Lord, and on his law he meditates day and night."

Nobody walks in the way of the wicked out of duty. Nobody stands in the way of sinners out of duty. Nobody sits in the seat of scoffers out of duty. We walk and stand and sit in their ways because that is what we want. And we want their ways because we have been watching them so intently that what they do has become attractive. We have, in one sense, meditated on them, and now we delight in them. We are shaped. That is how worldliness happens.

You start by looking at the stuff of the world and its

ways. You chase the distractions and hear the empty promises. But then you look at them and begin to think about them so much that you desire their ways, and therefore you find yourself walking and standing and sitting in their counsel, their ways, and their seats. Eventually you wake up to realize that you are dangerously similar to them.

That's why the contrast in verse 2 refers not to duty and obedience, but to delight and meditation. The point is that the only hope against the fleeting pleasure of the world is the lasting pleasure of God's truth. Just as the pleasures of the world are awakened by looking at them long enough, so the pleasures of God's truth are awakened in the born-again soul by fixing our hearts and mind on Scripture—day and night.

Meditate day and night on the instruction of God in the Psalms, the psalmist tells us, and delight will be awakened. That is what the Psalms are designed to do: *inform your thinking in a way that delights your heart*. Meditating day and night on God's truth leads to delighting, which then frees us from the fleeting pleasures of the wicked, the sinner and the scoffer.

So the very first two verses in the entire book of Psalms confirm what we have seen: this book is designed to shape our thinking through meditation, and shape our feeling through delight.

2. Why Does Verse 3 Read Like It Does?

Now here is the second question for Psalm 1 that turns up our second observation about this psalm. Why doesn't verse 3 say: "And when you meditate on God's instruction in the Psalms and delight in what you see, then you will not act wickedly and you will not act sinfully, and you will not scoff"? That would have rounded things out nicely with verse 1.

The answer is that the psalmist wants us to see that the life of the godly is like a tree bearing fruit, not like a laborer picking fruit. To use Paul's language, the Christian life is the fruit of the Spirit, not the works of the law. Verse 3 tells us, "He is like a tree planted by streams of water that yields its fruit in its season, and its leaf does not wither. In all that he does, he prospers."

Here is the picture of the Christian life: streams of water. The life of God flows through the Word of God, the Psalms, and God's sovereign grace plants you by these streams (see Matthew 15:13). Your roots reach deep into the water of life. Your leaves are green during the drought, and your life is fruitful when others' lives are barren.

The root system is not mechanical or automatic. The roots work by meditation—when you give focused attention and thought to the Psalms. That is where the roots meet the water. The result is delight—spiritual pleasure in what we see of God and his ways—and from this delight comes all kinds of transformed attitudes and behaviors. This is how we are changed.

The battle to avoid the counsel of the wicked and the way of the sinner and the seat of the scoffer—the battle to be righteous and holy and humble—is a fight that is won by delight. And that delight is nourished through meditating on God's instruction in the Psalms day and night.[2]

3. How Does Psalm 1 Lead Us to the Messiah?

One final question to ask of Psalm 1 is what it tells us about Jesus. How does this psalm lead us to the Messiah?

Right away, the word *righteous* in verse 6 presses us forward to Christ as our righteousness. "The LORD knows the way of the righteous, but the way of the wicked will perish." Only the righteous will survive the judgment in the end. So our question becomes: Who is righteous?

Psalm 14:3 tells us, "They have all turned aside; together they have become corrupt; there is none who does good, not even one." Psalm 130:3 asks rhetorically, "If you, O LORD, should mark iniquities, O Lord, who could stand?" Then there is Psalm 32:2, "Blessed is the man against whom the LORD counts no iniquity."

So "the righteous" are the sinful who can somehow be counted as righteous when they are not righteous in themselves. How can this be? How can a holy and righteous God *not* mark iniquity? How can a holy and righteous God *not* count sin? How can he *not* require perfect righteousness for his perfect heaven?

The answer is that God *does* mark iniquity, and he *does* count sin, and he *does* require perfect righteousness. And that is why this psalm, with all the Psalms, leads to Jesus who "was pierced for our transgressions; [and] crushed for our iniquities" (Isaiah 53:5). God *did* count our sin, and he punished it in Christ. He *did* require righteousness, and he manifested it in Christ. Romans 10:4 tells us that the goal of the law [the goal of the Psalms] is Christ, "for righteousness to everyone who believes."

This gospel truth is central to the living water that flows into the roots of our lives. This truth is what we meditate on day and night when we read and sing the Psalms. This is the source of our sweetest delight.

Embrace This Gospel River

I urge you to embrace this gospel as the river of your life, and I invite you to use this book as a means to learn with

me how to think and feel in tune with the Psalms. May
God shape us—our thinking and our feeling—so that we
bear the fruit of Christ-exalting love, joy, peace, patience,
kindness, goodness, faithfulness, gentleness, and self-con-
trol (Galatians 5:22–23).

PSALM 42

To the choirmaster. A maskil of the sons of Korah.

As a deer pants for flowing streams,
so pants my soul for you, O God.
My soul thirsts for God, for the living God.
When shall I come and appear before God?
My tears have been my food day and night,
while they say to me all the day long,
"Where is your God?"
These things I remember,
as I pour out my soul:
how I would go with the throng
and lead them in procession to the house of God
with glad shouts and songs of praise,
a multitude keeping festival.

Why are you cast down, O my soul,
and why are you in turmoil within me?
Hope in God; for I shall again praise him,
my salvation and my God.

My soul is cast down within me;
therefore I remember you
from the land of Jordan and of Hermon,
from Mount Mizar.
Deep calls to deep at the roar of your waterfalls;
all your breakers and your waves
have gone over me.
By day the Lord commands his steadfast love,
and at night his song is with me,
a prayer to the God of my life.
I say to God, my rock: "Why have you forgotten me?
Why do I go mourning
because of the oppression of the enemy?"
As with a deadly wound in my bones,
my adversaries taunt me,
while they say to me all the day long,
"Where is your God?"

Why are you cast down, O my soul,
and why are you in turmoil within me?
Hope in God; for I shall again praise him,
my salvation and my God.

2
Spiritual Depression

PSALM 42

The heading of this psalm reads: "To the choirmaster. A Maskil of the sons of Korah."

The sons of Korah were a group of priests who were charged with the ministry of singing. Second Chronicles 20:19 describes them in action: "The Korahites, stood up to praise the LORD, the God of Israel, with a very loud voice."

The heading of Psalm 42, therefore, implies that this psalm was probably sung in public worship. This is in line with what we saw in the introduction. The Psalms are songs. They are poems. They are written to awaken and express and shape the emotional life of God's people. Poetry and singing exist because God made us with emotions, not just thoughts. So our emotions are massively important.

The second thing to notice in the heading is that the psalm is called a *maskil*. It's not entirely clear what this word means, which is why most Bible translations simply use the transliteration of the Hebrew. *Maskil* comes from a Hebrew verb that means "to make someone wise," or "to instruct." When applied to the Psalms, it may mean a song that instructs, or a song that is wisely crafted. This idea of instruction is also in line with what we saw in the introduction. The Psalms are not only for the mind, but also for the heart. The Psalms intend to instruct, and instruction is ultimately a matter of the heart—the organ of delight. "Blessed is the man... [whose] *delight* is in the [instruction] of the LORD, and on his [instruction] he meditates day and night" (Psalm 1:1–2).

So this superscript, "To the choirmaster. A Maskil of the Sons of Korah," reiterates what we've already seen. The Psalms are instruction *and* songs. They are instruction and songs that have been inspired by God, intending to shape what the mind thinks and what the heart feels. When we immerse ourselves in the Psalms, we are being shaped by God.

Psalm 42: Fighting for Hope in God

The godly man of Psalm 42 is in the middle of unspecified oppressing circumstances. Verse 3 says that his enemies "say to me all the day long, 'Where is your God?'" And verse 10 says the same thing, only it describes the effect as a deadly wound: "As with a deadly wound in my bones, my adversaries taunt me, while they say to me all the day long, 'Where is your God?'" This taunt affirms the overall tone of the psalm that something has gone terribly wrong—so wrong that the taunters believe that the psalmist has been abandoned by God.

This apparent abandonment describes the external condition of the psalmist, but his internal emotional condition is no better. The psalmist is depressed and full of turmoil. In verses 5 and 11, he describes himself as "cast down" and "in turmoil." In verse 3, he says, "My tears have been my food day and night." He is discouraged to the point of continual crying. In verse 7, he says that he feels as if he were drowning: "All your breakers and your waves have gone over me."

In all of this, though, the psalmist is fighting for hope. Twice in this psalm, in the middle (v. 5) and in the conclusion (v. 11), he encourages himself using precisely the same language: "Why are you cast down, O my soul, and why are you in turmoil within me? Hope in God; for I shall again praise him, my salvation and my God." He is not surrendering to the emotions of discouragement. He is fighting back.

I cannot tell you how many hundreds of times in my pastoral ministry at Bethlehem Baptist Church I had to fight back the heaviness of discouragement with these very words: "Hope in God, John. Hope in God. You will again praise him." These verses were so central to our way of thinking and talking in the early 1980s that we put a huge "Hope in God" sign on the outside wall of the old sanctuary. We became known around the neighborhood as the "Hope in God" church, and to this very day, forty years later, these three words are used as our website URL.

Bittersweet Ending

The psalmist's external circumstances are oppressive, and his internal emotional condition is depressed and full of turmoil. But he is fighting for hope. And the truly remarkable thing, as we have just seen, is that at the end of the psalm he is still fighting for hope and not yet where he wants to be.

Is that a happy ending?

Like most things in this life, the conclusion is mixed. The faith of the psalmist is amazing, and his fight is valiant. But, then again, he is not where he wants to be in hope and peace and praise. Now, this psalm is in the Bible by God's design. Therefore, I assume that if we listen carefully, if we watch this psalmist struggle, if we meditate on this instruction day and night, then our *thoughts* about God and life, on the one hand, and our *emotions*, on the other hand, will be shaped by God. We will become more like a tree that bears fruit and whose leaves don't wither when the drought of oppression and discouragement and turmoil comes (Psalm 1:3). Examine with me the psalmist's responses to his inner turmoil.

How the Psalmist Responds to Discouragement

There are six ways the psalmist responds to the discouragement and turmoil that has come upon him. I'll list them in an order that they might have happened, though they surely overlap and repeat themselves.[3] These six things show us what a godly person does in the midst of spiritual depression, and I think they are meant to shape how we deal with our own seasons of darkness.

1. He Asks God Why

> *I say to God, my rock: "Why have you forgotten me?*
> *Why do I go mourning because of the oppression of*
> *the enemy?"* (Psalm 42:9)

First, the psalmist responds to his circumstances at one
point by asking God, "Why?" In this verse, *forgotten* is an
overstatement, and the psalmist knows it. He has just said
in the previous verse, "By day the LORD commands his
steadfast love, and at night his song is with me" (v. 8).

What he means is that it *looks* like God has forgotten him. It *feels* as if God has forgotten him. If God hasn't
forgotten him, he wonders, why aren't these enemies driven
back and consumed? It would be good if all of us were so
composed and careful in the expression of our discourage-
ments that we never said anything amiss, but that is not the
way we are. At least, that is not how it usually goes. In the
tumult of our emotions, we are not careful with our words.

Early in my preaching ministry, when I preached
through the book of Job, this truth came home to us as
a church. For years afterward we developed a category
for hearing the words of a suffering person, rooted in the
words of Job 6:26, "Do you think that you can reprove
words, when the speech of a despairing man is wind?"
We called this category "words for the wind"—which
means, don't jump on the words of despairing people. Let
it go. They are in pain. Their words are often uncensored
emotions. There will be ample time to discern the deeper
convictions of the heart. Let the wind blow away the
ill-chosen words. They are words for the wind.

So the psalmist asks, "Why?"—and it's a legitimate
question. He may not have asked the question with theo-

logical or linguistic precision, but if he understands in time that he did not literally mean that God had forgotten him, we will let those words go. They will prove to be words for the wind.

2. He Affirms God's Sovereign Love

> *By day the LORD commands his steadfast love, and at night his song is with me, a prayer to the God of my life.* (Psalm 42:8)

Second, in the midst of the psalmist's discouragement, he affirms God's sovereign love for him. In verses 5 and 11, he calls God "my salvation and my God." And even though he says that it looks as if God has forgotten him, he never stops believing in the absolute sovereignty of God over all his adversity. So at the end of verse 7, he says, "All your breakers and your waves have gone over me." *Your* breakers and *your* waves have gone over me.

In other words, all the tumultuous, oppressing, and discouraging circumstances are the waves *of God*. The psalmist never loses this grip on the great truths about God. They are the ballast in his little boat of faith. They keep him from capsizing in the chaos of his emotions, and there are many who know this to be true in their own lives. Many Christians have learned that relief in the midst of suffering is nowhere to be found if God does not rule the wind and the waves. The psalmist affirms God's sovereign love for him in and through all the troubles.

3. He Sings!

*By day the LORD commands his steadfast love, and
at night his song is with me, a prayer to the God of
my life.* (Psalm 42:8)

Third, the psalmist sings to the Lord at night, pleading for
his life. This is not a song of jubilant hope. The psalmist
doesn't feel jubilant right now. He is *seeking* jubilant hope.
This is a prayer song and pleading song—a song "to the
God of my life." That is, a song pleading for his life.

But isn't it amazing that he is *singing* his prayer? My
guess is that this is where Psalm 42 came from. This very
psalm may be that nighttime prayer song. Not many of us
can compose songs when we are discouraged and weeping
day and night. That's why a singable psalter is good to keep
around, or perhaps a hymnbook full of gospel truths. For
example, Isaac Watts wrote these verses to be sung:

How long wilt Thou conceal Thy face?
My God, how long delay?
When shall I feel those heav'nly rays
That chase my fears away?
How long shall my poor laboring soul
Wrestle and toil in vain?
Thy word can all my foes control
And ease my raging pain.
(Watts, "Psalm 13")

The Psalter of 1912 contains these verses to be sung the way
the psalmist of Psalm 42 sang at night:

How long wilt Thou forget me,

O Lord, Thou God of grace?
How long shall fears beset me
While darkness hides Thy face?

How long shall griefs distress me
And turn my day to night?
How long shall foes oppress me
And triumph in their might?

O Lord my God, behold me
And hear mine earnest cries;
Lest sleep of death enfold me,
Enlighten Thou mine eyes;

Lest now my foe insulting
Should boast of his success,
And enemies exulting
Rejoice in my distress.
(*The Psalter*, "Psalm 22")

These are not jubilant songs, but they are songs! And they are songs of faith. They are shaped by thinking and feeling with God in the Psalms.

4. He Preaches to His Own Soul

Why are you cast down, O my soul, and why are you in turmoil within me? Hope in God; for I shall again praise him, my salvation and my God.
(Psalm 42:5)

Fourth, the psalmist preaches to his own soul. This is so crucial in the fight of faith. We must learn to preach the truth to ourselves. Martyn Lloyd-Jones writes,

Have you realized that most of your unhappiness
in life is due to the fact that you are listening
to yourself instead of talking to yourself? Take
those thoughts that come to you the moment
you wake up in the morning. You have not
originated them but they are talking to you, they
bring back the problems of yesterday, etc. Some-
body is talking. Who is talking to you? Your self
is talking to you. Now this man's treatment [in
Psalm 42] was this: instead of allowing this self
to talk to him, he starts talking to himself. "Why
art thou cast down, O my soul?" he asks. His
soul had been depressing him, crushing him. So
he stands up and says,: "Self, listen for a moment,
I will speak to you."[4]

On this side of the cross, we know the greatest ground for
our hope: Jesus Christ crucified for our sins and trium-
phant over death. So the main thing we must learn is to
preach this gospel to ourselves:

Listen, self: If God is for you, who can be against you?
He who did not spare his own Son but gave him up for
you, how will he not also with him graciously give you all
things? Who shall bring any charge against you as God's
elect? It is God who justifies. Who is to condemn? Christ
Jesus is the one who died—more than that, who was
raised—who is at the right hand of God, who indeed is
interceding for you. Who shall separate you from the love
of Christ? (Romans 8:31–35, paraphrased)

If this psalmist were living after Jesus's death and
resurrection, he would have said something like this. Let
us learn with the psalmist to preach the gospel to ourselves.

5. He Remembers Past Experiences

*These things I remember, as I pour out my soul: how
I would go with the throng and lead them in procession to the house of God with glad shouts and songs
of praise, a multitude keeping festival. (Psalm 42:4)*

Fifth, the psalmist remembers. He calls past experiences to
mind. He remembers past corporate worship experiences.

This speaks volumes about the importance of corporate worship in our lives. Don't take the significance
of those times lightly. What we do in corporate worship
with other Christians is a real transaction with the living
God. God means for these encounters with him in corporate worship to preserve our faith now, in a way that we
will remember later. If corporate worship were not a real
supernatural work of God, it would be pure sentimental-
ism for the psalmist to remember his experiences. He is
not engaging in nostalgia. He is confirming his faith in
the midst of turmoil and discouragement by remembering
how real God was in corporate worship.

6. He Thirsts for God

*As a deer pants for flowing streams, so pants my
soul for you, O God. My soul thirsts for God, for the
living God. When shall I come and appear before
God? (Psalm 42:1–2)*

Finally, the psalmist thirsts for God like a deer pants for
the stream. What makes this activity so beautiful, and so
crucial for us, is that he is not thirsting mainly for relief
from his threatening circumstances. He is not thirsting
mainly for escape from his enemies or for their destruction.

It's not wrong to want relief and to pray for it, and it is sometimes right to pray for the defeat of enemies, but more important than any of that is God himself. When we think and feel with God in the Psalms, this is the main result: we come to love God. We want to see God, and be with God, and be satisfied in admiring and exulting in God.

That is my ultimate hope and prayer for you in this short book. My aim is that God would be revealed, and that you would want to know him.

See God's Face in Christ's Gospel

A likely translation of the end of verse 2 is: "When will I come and see the face of God?" The final answer to that question was given in John 14:9 and 2 Corinthians 4:4. Jesus said, "Whoever has seen me has seen the Father" (John 14:9). And Paul said that when we are converted to Christ we see "the light of the gospel of the glory of Christ, who is the image of God" (2 Corinthians 4:4).

When we see the face of Christ, we see the face of God—and we see the glory of his face when we hear the story of the gospel of his death and resurrection. It is "the gospel of the glory of Christ, who is the image of God."

May God increase our hunger and thirst to see his face. And may he grant our desire to be fulfilled through the gospel of the glory of his Son, who is the image of God.

PSALM 51

To the choirmaster. A Psalm of David, when Nathan the
prophet went to him, after he had gone in to Bathsheba.

Have mercy on me, O God, according to your steadfast love;
according to your abundant mercy blot out my transgressions.
Wash me thoroughly from my iniquity,
and cleanse me from my sin!
For I know my transgressions, and my sin is ever before me.
Against you, you only, have I sinned
and done what is evil in your sight,
so that you may be justified in your words
and blameless in your judgment.
Behold, I was brought forth in iniquity,
and in sin did my mother conceive me.
Behold, you delight in truth in the inward being,
and you teach me wisdom in the secret heart.

Purge me with hyssop, and I shall be clean;
wash me, and I shall be whiter than snow.
Let me hear joy and gladness;
let the bones that you have broken rejoice.
Hide your face from my sins, and blot out all my iniquities.
Create in me a clean heart, O God,
and renew a right spirit within me.
Cast me not away from your presence,
and take not your Holy Spirit from me.
Restore to me the joy of your salvation,
and uphold me with a willing spirit.

Then I will teach transgressors your ways,
and sinners will return to you.
Deliver me from bloodguiltiness, O God, O God of my salvation,
and my tongue will sing aloud of your righteousness.
O Lord, open my lips, and my mouth will declare your praise.
For you will not delight in sacrifice, or I would give it;
you will not be pleased with a burnt offering.
The sacrifices of God are a broken spirit;
a broken and contrite heart, O God, you will not despise.

Do good to Zion in your good pleasure;
build up the walls of Jerusalem;
then will you delight in right sacrifices,
in burnt offerings and whole burnt offerings;
then bulls will be offered on your altar.

3

A Broken and Contrite Heart God Will Not Despise

PSALM 51

The previous chapter focused on how to be discouraged *in a godly way*, and now this chapter focuses on how to be crushed *in a way that honors God.* There is an intentional pattern here. What makes a person a Christian is not that he doesn't get discouraged, and not that he doesn't sin and feel miserable about it. What makes a person a Christian is *the connection he has with Jesus Christ.* That connection is what shapes how he thinks and feels about his discouragement and guilt.

The Psalms were the main songbook of the early church, and they were designed by God, centuries before, to awaken and express and shape the thoughts and feelings of Jesus's disciples. We learn from the Psalms how to think about discouragement and guilt, and we learn from the Psalms how to feel in times of discouragement and in times of horrible regret. The Psalms show us how to be discouraged well and how to feel regret well.

My prayer is that you will form the habit of living in the Psalms so much that the world of your thinking and the world of your feeling will be transformed into full-blooded biblical thinking and biblical feeling.

David's Fall and Forgiveness

Psalm 51 is one of the few psalms that are pinpointed as to their historical origin. The heading of the psalm is: "To the choirmaster. A Psalm of David, when Nathan the prophet went to him, after he had gone in to Bathsheba." What happened with Bathsheba is well-known. Here it is in crisp biblical words from 2 Samuel 11:2–5:

> It happened, late one afternoon, when David arose from his couch and was walking on the roof of the king's house, that he saw from the roof a woman bathing; and the woman was very beautiful. And David sent and inquired about the woman. And one said, "Is not this Bathsheba, the daughter of Eliam, the wife of Uriah the Hittite?" So David sent messengers and took her, and she came to him, and he lay with her…. Then she returned to her house. And the woman conceived, and she sent and told David, "I am pregnant."

David tried to cover his sin by bringing Uriah, Bathsheba's husband, home from battle so Uriah could sleep with her and think that the child was his. But Uriah was too noble to sleep with his wife while his comrades were in battle, so David arranged to have Uriah killed so that he could quickly marry Bathsheba and hide his sin.

In one of the most understated sentences of the Bible, the story ends with these words: "The thing that David had done displeased the LORD" (2 Samuel 11:27). Then God sends the prophet Nathan to David with a parable that entices David to pronounce his own condemnation. Nathan tells David, "You are the man!" (2 Samuel 12:7). Then Nathan asks, "Why have you despised the word of the LORD?" (2 Samuel 12:9). David breaks and confesses, "I have sinned against the LORD" (2 Samuel 12:13). Nathan replies, astonishingly, "The LORD also has put away your sin; you shall not die. Nevertheless, because by this deed you have utterly scorned the LORD, the child who is born to you shall die" (2 Samuel 12:13–14).

"The LORD Has Put Away Your Sin"

This is outrageous. Bathsheba has effectively been raped. Uriah is dead. The baby will die. And Nathan says, "The LORD has put away your sin." Just like that? David committed adultery—given his power as king, you might call it royal rape. He ordered murder. He lied. He "despised the word of the LORD." He "scorned the LORD." And then, astonishingly, it simply says that the Lord "put away [his] sin" (2 Samuel 12:13). What kind of a righteous judge is God? You don't just pass over rape and murder and lying and divine desecration. Righteous judges don't do that. None of us would approve a local county judge who did that in our city for a murder and rapist who happened to have a good lawyer.

We should all be outraged at God's behavior here— except for one thing. The apostle Paul shares our outrage and explains how God could be both just and the one who justifies murderers and rapists and liars and worse. Paul tells us in Romans 3:25–26. This is one of the most important sentences in the Bible for understanding how Jesus relates to the Psalms, and to the Old Testament in general:

> God put [Jesus] forward as a propitiation by his blood, to be received by faith. This was to show God's righteousness, because in his divine forbearance he had passed over former sins [that's exactly what 2 Samuel 12:13 says that God did—he passed over David's sin]. It was to show his righteousness at the present time, so that he might be just and the justifier of the one who has faith in Jesus.

In other words, the outrage we feel when God seems to simply pass over David's sin would be good outrage if God were simply sweeping David's sin under the rug. *But he is not.* God sees from the time of David, down through the centuries, to the death of his Son, who would die in David's place. So we see that *David's faith in God's merciful promise of a Messiah unites David with the Messiah.* And in God's all-knowing mind, David's sins are counted as Jesus's sins and Jesus's righteousness is counted as David's righteousness, and *that* is how God justly passes over David's sin.

God did not sweep sin under the rug of the universe and treat it lightly, as though it was no great outrage. He revealed the outrage by requiring the outrageous death of the innocent and infinitely worthy Son of God. Jesus said that he came to die to uphold and vindicate the glory of God which had been desecrated by sins like David's (and ours!): "What shall I say? 'Father, save me from this hour'? But for this purpose I have come to this hour. Father, glorify your name" (John 12:27–28).

When Jesus died, he openly declared and proved the

infinite value of the glory of God. This meant that God's passing over the glory-trampling sin of David was shown *not* to be an unjust dishonor to God. Jesus has made mercy just. He absorbed the wrath that David deserved, and vindicated the value of the glory of God that David despised.

Daily Appropriating Forgiveness

The death of Jesus is the objective reality of how David is forgiven for his sin and justified in the presence of God. But what Psalm 51 describes is what David *felt* and *thought* as he laid hold on God's mercy. Some might say that Christians, because of the death of Jesus, should not pray and confess as David does in this Psalm. I don't think that's right.

To be sure, Jesus purchased our forgiveness and provided our righteousness once for all, by his life and death. We can add nothing to the purchase or the provision. We share in the forgiveness and the righteousness by faith alone.

However, in view of the holiness of God and the evil of sin, it is fitting that we appropriate and apply what he bought for us by prayer and confession every day. "Give us this day our daily bread, and forgive us our debts, as we also have forgiven our debtors" (Matthew 6:11–12). We make a daily request for bread, because he has promised to meet every need; and we make a daily prayer to appropriate God's forgiveness, because he has fully purchased and secured it for us by the death of Jesus.

David's Responses to His Sin

Psalm 51 is the way that God's people should think and feel about the horrors of their own sin. This is a psalm

about how be crushed well for our sin. I will try to guide
you through four of David's responses to his own sin.

1. He Turns to God

*Have mercy on me, O God, according to your stead-
fast love; according to your abundant mercy blot out
my transgressions.* (Psalm 51:1)

First, David turns to his only hope, the mercy and love
of God. He appeals to God three times: "Have mercy,"
"according to your steadfast love," and "according to your
abundant mercy." This is what God had promised in
Exodus 34:6–7: "The LORD, the LORD, a God merciful
and gracious, slow to anger, and abounding in steadfast
love and faithfulness, keeping steadfast love for thousands,
forgiving iniquity and transgression and sin, but who will
by no means clear the guilty."

David knew that there were guilty sinners who
would not be forgiven. And there were guilty sinners who,
by some mysterious work of redemption, would not be
counted as guilty, but instead would be forgiven. Psalm 51
is David's way of laying hold of that mystery of mercy.

We know more of the mystery of this redemption
than David did—*we know Jesus*—but we lay hold of the
mercy in the same way he did. David turned helpless to
the mercy and love of God. We turn helpless to the mercy
and love of God *through Jesus.*

2. He Prays for Cleansing

*Wash me thoroughly from my iniquity, and cleanse
me from my sin.... Purge me with hyssop, and I*

shall be clean; wash me, and I shall be whiter than
snow. (Psalm 51:2, 7)

Second, David prays for cleansing from his sin. What is the point of referring to "hyssop"? When a house had a disease in it, and steps were taken to successfully rid the house of the disease, *hyssop* was the branch used by the priests to sprinkle blood on the house and declare it clean (Leviticus 14:51). David is crying out to God, as his ultimate priest, to forgive him and count him clean from his sin.

It is fitting that Christians also ask God for cleansing (1 John 1:7–9). Jesus has purchased our forgiveness. He has paid the full price for it. His finished work, however, does not *replace* our asking—it is the basis for our asking. It is the reason we are confident that the answer will be yes. First, David looks helplessly to the mercy of God. Second, he prays that God in his mercy would forgive him and make him clean.

3. He Confesses the Seriousness of His Sin

For I know my transgressions, and my sin is ever
before me. Against you, you only, have I sinned and
done what is evil in your sight, so that you may
be justified in your words and blameless in your
judgment. Behold, I was brought forth in iniquity,
and in sin did my mother conceive me. Behold, you
delight in truth in the inward being, and you teach
me wisdom in the secret heart. (Psalm 51:3-6)

Third, David confesses at least five ways that his sin is extremely serious.

The Sin Is Emblazoned on His Conscience

David says that he can't get the sin out of his mind. Verse
3: "For I know my transgressions, and my sin is ever before
me." *Ever* before him. At a minimum, he retains a vivid
awareness of the awfulness of his sin. Perhaps the scene
itself keeps playing over and over in his mind. In any event,
he can't shake it.

His Sin Is Mainly against God

Nathan said that David despised God and scorned his
word. So David says in verse 4: "Against you, you only,
have I sinned and done what is evil in your sight." This
doesn't mean that Bathsheba and Uriah and the baby
weren't hurt. It means that what makes sin to be sin is that
sin is *against God*. Hurting man is bad. It is horribly bad.
But that's not the greatest horror of sin. Sin is ultimately
an attack on God—a belittling of God. David admits this
in striking terms: "Against you, you only, have I sinned."

He Vindicates God, Not Himself

There is no self-justification. No defense. No escape. Verse
4: "so that you may be justified in your words and blameless in your judgment." God is justified. God is blameless.
If God casts David into hell, God will be innocent. This
is radical, God-centered repentance. This is the way that
redeemed people think and feel. God would be just to
damn us, and the simple fact that we are still breathing is
sheer mercy. The fact that we are *forgiven* is pure, blood-
bought mercy. David vindicates the righteousness of God,
not himself.

He Draws Attention to His Inborn Corruption

Verse 5: "Behold, I was brought forth in iniquity, and in
sin did my mother conceive me." Some people use their

inborn or inbred corruption to diminish their sense of personal guilt. David uses it to intensify his guilt. For him, the fact that he committed adultery, committed murder, and lied, are expressions of something worse: he is *by nature* an adulterer, a murderer, and a liar. If God does not rescue him, he will do more and more evil.

He Admits He Sinned against God's Merciful Light in His Heart

Verse 6: "Behold, you delight in truth in the inward being, and you teach me wisdom in the secret heart." God had been David's teacher. God had made him wise, and David had done many wise things. And then sin got the upper hand. For David, this made it all the worse: *I have been blessed with so much knowledge and so much wisdom. Oh how deep must be my depravity that it could rise up and sin against so much light!*

So David joins the prophet Nathan, and God, in condemning his sin and confessing the depths of his corruption.

4. He Pleads for Renewal

> *Let me hear joy and gladness; let the bones that you have broken rejoice....Create in me a clean heart, O God, and renew a right spirit within me. Cast me not away from your presence, and take not your Holy Spirit from me. Restore to me the joy of your salvation, and uphold me with a willing spirit. Then I will teach transgressors your ways, and sinners will return to you....O Lord, open my lips, and my mouth will declare your praise....The sacrifices of God are a broken spirit; a broken and contrite heart, O God, you will not despise.* (Psalm 51: 8, 10-13, 15, 17)

Finally, after turning helpless to God's mercy, and praying for forgiveness and cleansing, and confessing the depth and greatness of his sin and corruption, David pleads for more than forgiveness. He pleads for renewal. He is passionately committed to being changed by God.

David pours out his heart for this change in at least six ways. I can only draw your attention to them. The main point is: *forgiven people are committed to being changed by God.* The adulterer, the murderer, and the liar, when they experience God's forgiveness, hate what they were, and yearn to be changed by God.

He Prays That God Would Confirm to Him His Election

Verse 11: "Cast me not away from your presence, and take not your Holy Spirit from me." Some say that the elect should not pray like this because it implies that you can lose your salvation, but I disagree.

When David or I pray, "Don't cast me away, and don't take your Spirit from me," we mean: *Don't treat me as one who is not chosen. Don't let me prove to be like one of those in Hebrews 6 who have only tasted the Holy Spirit. Don't let me fall away and show that I was only drawn by the Spirit, and not held by the Spirit. Confirm to me, O God, that I am your child and will never fall away.*

He Prays for a Heart and a Spirit That are New and Right and Firm

Verse 10: "Create in me a clean heart, O God, and renew a right spirit within me." The "right spirit" here is the established, firm, unwavering spirit. He wants to be done with the kind of instability he has just experienced.

He Prays for a Willing Spirit and the Joy of God's Salvation

Verse 8: "Let me hear joy and gladness; let the bones that

you have broken rejoice." Verse 12: "Restore to me the joy of your salvation, and uphold me with a willing spirit."

It is astonishing that in this Psalm, David never prays directly about sex. His corruption all started with sex, leading to deceit, leading to murder…or did it? I don't think so.

Why isn't he crying out for sexual restraint? Why isn't he praying for men to hold him accountable? Why isn't he praying for protected eyes and lust-free thoughts? The reason is that David knows that sexual sin is a symptom, not the disease. People give way to sexual sin because they don't have fullness of joy and gladness in Jesus. Their spirits are not steadfast and firm and established. They waver. They are enticed, and they give way because God does not have the proper place in their feelings and thoughts.

David knew this about himself. It's true about us, too. Through the words of his prayer, David shows us the real need for those who sin sexually. This psalm does not contain a single word about sex. Instead, David prays: "Let me hear joy and gladness; let the bones that you have broken rejoice.…Restore to me the joy of your salvation, and uphold me with a willing [firm, established] spirit" (vv. 8, 12). David cries out for a spirit that is joyfully willing to follow God. David wants to be generous with people rather than exploiting people. His prayer is profound wisdom for us.

He Asks God to Cause His Joy to Overflow into Praise

Verse 15: "O Lord, open my lips, and my mouth will declare your praise." Praise is what joy in God does when obstacles are taken out of the way. That is what he is praying for: *O God, overcome everything in my life that keeps my heart dull and my mouth shut, when I ought to be praising you. Make my joy irrepressible.*

He Asks That the Upshot of All This Will Be a Life of Effective Witness

Verse 13: "Then I will teach transgressors your ways, and sinners will return to you." David is not content to be forgiven. He is not content to be clean. He is not content to be elect. He is not content to have a right spirit. He is not content to be joyful in God by himself. He will not be content until his broken life serves the healing of others. "Then I will teach transgressors your ways, and sinners will return to you."

He Discovers Something Vital

Under all of this, David has discovered that God has crushed him in love, and that a broken and contrite heart is the mark of all God's children. Verse 17: "The sacrifices of God are a broken spirit; a broken and contrite heart, O God, you will not despise."

Brokenhearted Joy

This is foundational to everything. Being a Christian means being broken and contrite. Don't make the mistake of thinking that you get beyond that in this life. Brokenness marks the life of God's happy children until they die. We are broken and contrite all the way home—unless sin gets the proud upper hand. Being broken and contrite is not *against* joy and praise and witness. It is the *flavor* of Christian joy and praise and witness. Jonathan Edwards says it best:

All gracious affections [feelings, emotions] that
are a sweet [aroma] to Christ... are brokenhearted affections. A truly Christian love, either
to God or men, is a humble brokenhearted love.
The desires of the saints, however earnest, are
humble desires: their hope is a humble hope;
and their joy, even when it is unspeakable, and
full of glory, is a humble broken-hearted joy.[5]

PSALM 103

Of David.

Bless the Lord, O my soul,
and all that is within me, bless his holy name!
Bless the Lord, O my soul, and forget not all his benefits,
who forgives all your iniquity, who heals all your diseases,
who redeems your life from the pit,
who crowns you with steadfast love and mercy,
who satisfies you with good
so that your youth is renewed like the eagle's.

The Lord works righteousness
and justice for all who are oppressed.
He made known his ways to Moses, his acts to the people of Israel.
The Lord is merciful and gracious,
slow to anger and abounding in steadfast love.
He will not always chide, nor will he keep his anger forever.
He does not deal with us according to our sins,
nor repay us according to our iniquities.
For as high as the heavens are above the earth,
so great is his steadfast love toward those who fear him;
as far as the east is from the west,
so far does he remove our transgressions from us.
As a father shows compassion to his children,
so the Lord shows compassion to those who fear him.
For he knows our frame; he remembers that we are dust.

As for man, his days are like grass;
he flourishes like a flower of the field;
for the wind passes over it, and it is gone,
and its place knows it no more.
But the steadfast love of the Lord
is from everlasting to everlasting on those who fear him,
and his righteousness to children's children,
to those who keep his covenant
and remember to do his commandments.
The Lord has established his throne in the heavens,
and his kingdom rules over all.

Bless the Lord, O you his angels,
you mighty ones who do his word, obeying the voice of his word!
Bless the Lord, all his hosts, his ministers, who do his will!
Bless the Lord, all his works, in all places of his dominion.
Bless the Lord, O my soul!

4

Bless the Lord, O My Soul

PSALM 103

Having been instructed from Psalm 42 about spiritual depression, and from Psalm 51 about regret and guilt, we turn now to Psalm 103 and the giving of gratitude and praise to God for his goodness. While this Psalm is for all believers, it is particularly relevant for parents, especially fathers. Accordingly, while much of this chapter will emphasize the role of fathers, Psalm 103 provides all believers with powerful instruction for how we should think, feel, and act in response to God's mercy, goodness, and compassion.

Faithful Fatherhood Blesses God Continually

When Verse 13 of Psalm 103 says, "As a father shows compassion to his children, so the LORD shows compassion to those who fear him," it does not mean that the

Lord learns how to be God by watching human fathers. It does not mean that God wonders whether he should be compassionate and then notices that good fathers are compassionate and so he decides to act compassionately, too.

Rather, verse 13 means that when you see a good father, you are seeing a picture of God. Or to put it another way, *God designed human fatherhood to be a portrait of himself.* God had a Son before he created Adam. He was God the Father before he was God the Creator. He knew what he wanted to portray before he created the portrayal. *love this*

The clear implication for all fathers is that we were designed to display the fatherhood of God—especially (but not only) to our children. And that implies that we learn to be fathers by watching God care for his children. It also implies that children learn what God's fatherhood is like largely by watching *us*.

We Are as Dust

So the chain of influence moves from God—the infinitely perfect Father of his imperfect children, who demonstrates good fatherhood—to us, so that in turn we can show our children and others what God's fatherhood is like. That is the calling of a father. When David says, "As a father shows compassion to his children, so the LORD shows compassion to those who fear him" (v. 13), he means that *God created fatherhood in his own image, and good fathering points to God.*

When David says in verse 14 that fathers (and the rest of us) are like dust ("[God] knows our frame; he remembers that we are dust"), it causes David to reflect on the shortness of human life and the never-beginning, never-ending life of God, and how that relates to our children.

> As for man, his days are like grass;
> he flourishes like a flower of the field;
> for the wind passes over it, and it is gone,
> and its place knows it no more.
> But the steadfast love of the LORD is from ever-
> lasting to everlasting on those who fear him,
> and his righteousness to children's children,
> to those who keep his covenant
> and remember to do his commandments.
> (vv. 15–18)

Fathers need to realize that they won't always be around, and their children won't always be around. Verse 17 refers to the "children's children." So the question a father should ask is, *How can my children benefit forever from the love of God? How can those children become the beneficiaries of God's righteousness, rather than being condemned by it?*

Verses 17–18 give three answers to that question. The steadfast love of God and the righteousness of God will follow your children from generation to generation if three things happen:

1. if they fear him (v. 17);
2. if they keep his covenant (v. 18);
3. if they do his commandments (v. 18).

Keeping God's Covenant Today

Let's focus for just a moment on that second requirement: "His righteousness [is shown] to children's children, to those who keep his covenant" (vv. 17–18). What does keeping the covenant of God mean today?

Things have changed since the Messiah has come. At the Last Supper, Jesus lifted up the cup representing his own blood and said, "This cup that is poured out for you is the *new covenant* in my blood" (Luke 22:20).

There is now a new covenant between God and his people, and this new covenant provides the blood of Christ to cover our sins and the power of the Spirit to enable us to walk in newness of life. The new covenant requires that we be united to Jesus by the new birth and that we receive Jesus as our Savior and Lord and treasure.

So when verses 17–18 say that the love and righteousness of God will bless our children if they keep God's covenant, it means that today our children must receive Jesus as the supremely valuable Savior and Lord of their lives.

The other two conditions David mentions for receiving God's steadfast love and righteous care are fearing God (v. 17) and doing his commandments (v. 18).

Fearing God *Means we run to Him not from Him.*

Verse 17: "The steadfast love of the LORD is from everlasting to everlasting on those who fear him." Fearing God means that God is so powerful and so holy and so awesome to us that we would not dare to run away from him, but only run to him for all that he promises to be for us. Fearing God is not the opposite from coming to the Messiah, Jesus. It's the *way* we come. We come reverently. We come humbly. We come without presuming that God owes us anything. We come trembling, broken, and contrite—fearing that our fickle hearts will turn away unless he takes hold of us and keeps us.

Doing His Commandments

The third condition David mentions (in order for our children to experience God's righteousness as saving, not condemning) is in verse 18: "to those who... remember to do his commandments." This means that faith in the redeemer must be real—*real* trust in Christ, *real* submission to his rule, and *real* treasuring of his worth: these things actually change our lives. So the requirement of obedience in verse 18 is simply the requirement that our fear of God and our trust in Christ be effective and fruitful. The blood and righteousness of Jesus alone is what forgives and justifies us, but it's our obedience, however imperfect, which *shows* that God has saved us. Our obedience *shows* that our faith is real, that we are truly covenant keepers, that we hold fast to our treasured substitute, Jesus Christ.

So fathers, know that we are like dust. We are like grass. We flourish like the flower of the field. The wind passes over it and it is gone, and its place knows it no more (vv. 15–16). After us come our children and their children, and the question for us now is: Will they fear God? Will they keep his covenant? Will they do his commandments?

If they do, the steadfast love of God and the righteousness of God will bless them forever.

Let Us Bless the Lord

What then is the one thing this psalm stresses, more than anything else, that parents, especially fathers, should do in leading our children to this condition of blessedness? What is the one main thing that this psalm calls all of us to do for our families and friends? For our churches? For our cities? For our own souls? The answer is relevant to everyone.

The answer is: *bless the Lord.*

The psalm begins and ends with the psalmist preaching to his soul to bless the Lord—and preaching to the angels and the hosts of heaven and the works of God's hands. The psalm is overwhelmingly focused on blessing the Lord.

Verses 1–2: "Bless the Lord, O my soul, and all that is within me, bless his holy name! Bless the Lord, O my soul, and forget not all his benefits." Then he starts listing the benefits. At the end, in verses 20–22, he concludes the list:

> Bless the Lord, O you his angels,
> you mighty ones who do his word,
> obeying the voice of his word!
> Bless the Lord, all his hosts,
> his ministers, who do his will!
> Bless the Lord, all his works,
> in all places of his dominion.
> Bless the Lord, O my soul!"

What does it mean to bless the Lord? *It means to speak well of God's greatness and goodness.* It is almost synonymous with praise. Psalm 34:1 puts them together like this: "I will bless the Lord at all times; his praise shall continually be in my mouth." Notice the word *mouth*: "His praise shall continually be in my mouth." Blessing the Lord means *speaking* or *singing* about the goodness and greatness of the Lord.

David is saying, in the first and last verses of this psalm, that speaking about God's goodness and greatness must come from the soul. Blessing God with the mouth, without the soul, would be hypocrisy. Jesus said, "This people honors me with their lips, but their heart is far from me" (Matthew 15:8). David knows the danger of that hypocrisy, and he is preaching to himself that it will not happen. In effect, he says to himself: *Come, soul, look at the greatness and goodness of God. Join my mouth, and let us bless the Lord with our whole being.*

As parents, perhaps the most effective thing we can do to help our children trust God is to bless the Lord continually in their presence. And to do it authentically, from our souls.

Three Reasons to Bless the Lord

We could take several more chapters in this little book to unpack all the reasons David assembles for why his soul should bless the Lord. Psalm 103 is one of the most gospel-rich psalms in the entire book. For now, though, I will only mention three reasons why David, and we, should bless the Lord.

1. God Is Sovereign

First, we should bless the Lord for his sovereignty. Verse 19: "The LORD has established his throne in the heavens, and his kingdom rules over all." Let our children hear us say, "I bless you, Lord, that your kingdom rules over all." God rules over all—all people, all governments, all weather systems, all animals, all molecules, all galaxies.

David knows that God exercises his sovereign rule through angels and heavenly beings, so he calls them to join him in his blessing (vv. 20–22). In effect, he says: "Come, angels, bless the Lord as you do his word. Come, hosts of heaven, bless the Lord as you do his will. Come, all you works of his hands everywhere in his dominion, bless the Lord!"

2. God Is Righteous and Just

Second, we should bless the Lord for his justice and righteousness. Verse 6: "The LORD works righteousness and justice for all who are oppressed." Let our children hear us exult in the righteous advocacy of God for the oppressed. At the dinner table, and in family devotions, we should say things like, "We bless you, O God, for your justice and your righteousness. We bless you that though the wrong seem oft so strong, your righteousness will reign. We bless you that justice will be done in this age or the next. Bless the Lord!"

3. God Is Merciful and Forgiving

Finally, we should bless the Lord for his mercy and his forgiveness. If this psalm celebrates anything clearly, it is the immeasurable mercy of God not to hold our sins against us. This is the gospel. We know that it is all owing to Jesus. Sweeter words have hardly been penned:

> Bless the LORD…
> who forgives all your iniquity… [for]
> he does not deal with us according to our sins,
> nor repay us according to our iniquities.
> For as high as the heavens are above the earth, so
> great is his steadfast love

toward those who fear him;
as far as the east is from the west,
so far does he remove our transgressions from us.
(vv. 2–3, 10–12)

Fathers, let your children hear you bless the Lord for the
gospel. Let them hear your soul exult in Jesus. Let them
hear your humble heart leap up with gratitude that your
sins—yes mommy's and daddy's sins—are forgiven. Let
them hear your affections for the Savior. Let them hear
you say, "Lord, I bless your name that my guilt is taken
away!" Then love your wife and children the way Jesus
loved you.

PSALM 69

To the choirmaster. According to the Lilies. Of David.

Save me, O God!
For the waters have come up to my neck.
I sink in deep mire,
where there is no foothold;
I have come into deep waters,
and the flood sweeps over me.
I am weary with my crying out;
my throat is parched.
My eyes grow dim
with waiting for my God.

More in number than the hairs of my head
are those who hate me without cause;
mighty are those who would destroy me,
those who attack me with lies.
What I did not steal
must I now restore?
O God, you know my folly;
the wrongs I have done are not hidden from you.

Let not those who hope in you be put to shame through me,
O Lord God of hosts;
let not those who seek you be brought to dishonor through me,
O God of Israel.
For it is for your sake that I have borne reproach,
that dishonor has covered my face.
I have become a stranger to my brothers,
an alien to my mother's sons.

For zeal for your house has consumed me,
and the reproaches of those who reproach you have fallen on me.
When I wept and humbled my soul with fasting,
it became my reproach.
When I made sackcloth my clothing,
I became a byword to them.
I am the talk of those who sit in the gate,
and the drunkards make songs about me.

But as for me, my prayer is to you, O LORD.
At an acceptable time, O God,
in the abundance of your steadfast love
answer me in your saving faithfulness.
Deliver me
from sinking in the mire;
let me be delivered from my enemies
and from the deep waters.
Let not the flood sweep over me,
or the deep swallow me up,
or the pit close its mouth over me.

Answer me, O LORD, for your steadfast love is good;
according to your abundant mercy, turn to me.
Hide not your face from your servant;
for I am in distress; make haste to answer me.
Draw near to my soul, redeem me;
ransom me because of my enemies!

You know my reproach,
and my shame and my dishonor;
my foes are all known to you.
Reproaches have broken my heart,
so that I am in despair.
I looked for pity, but there was none,
and for comforters, but I found none.
They gave me poison for food,
and for my thirst they gave me sour wine to drink.

Let their own table before them become a snare;
and when they are at peace, let it become a trap.
Let their eyes be darkened, so that they cannot see,
and make their loins tremble continually.
Pour out your indignation upon them,
and let your burning anger overtake them.
May their camp be a desolation;
let no one dwell in their tents.
For they persecute him whom you have struck down,
and they recount the pain of those you have wounded.
Add to them punishment upon punishment;

may they have no acquittal from you.
Let them be blotted out of the book of the living;
let them not be enrolled among the righteous.

But I am afflicted and in pain;
let your salvation, O God, set me on high!

I will praise the name of God with a song;
I will magnify him with thanksgiving.
This will please the LORD more than an ox
or a bull with horns and hoofs.
When the humble see it they will be glad;
you who seek God, let your hearts revive.
For the LORD hears the needy
and does not despise his own people who are prisoners.

Let heaven and earth praise him,
the seas and everything that moves in them.
For God will save Zion
and build up the cities of Judah,
and people shall dwell there and possess it;
the offspring of his servants shall inherit it,
and those who love his name shall dwell in it.

5

Pour Out Your Indignation upon Them

PSALM 69

As we have seen, the Psalms are inspired by God, and are therefore meant to instruct us about how to think about God and human nature and life. The Psalms are also poems that are meant to awaken and express and shape our feelings about God and human nature and life.

In previous chapters, we focused on spiritual depression (Psalm 42), on regret and guilt (Psalm 51), and on gratitude and praise (Psalm 103). This chapter focuses on the emotion of anger, specifically the desire for retaliation or vengeance—the anger we feel when something happens that is horribly wrong or unjust.

When great evil and injustice are portrayed in a film, and the antagonists seem to be getting away with it, we bristle with anger. But then, when some noble, humble, sacrificial character risks his life, captures the villains, and brings them to justice, we feel a deep satisfaction. Is it good that we have this feeling?

Even in our own lives, we are often bitterly opposed and sometimes horribly treated. Our hearts cry out for justice, for the punishment of our adversaries. How should we feel about those who have wronged us—perhaps terribly wronged us? How should we feel, and how should we think? What should we do?

Psalms That Curse

There is a group of psalms known as imprecatory psalms because they include imprecations, or curses, against God's enemies. These psalms are often seen as posing problems for Christians because Jesus taught us, "Love your enemies, do good to those who hate you, bless those who curse you, pray for those who abuse you" (Luke 6:27–28). And Jesus prayed for his enemies on the cross, "Father, forgive them, for they know not what they do" (Luke 23:34). It sounds like these psalms are doing the opposite of what Jesus said and did.

For example, let's consider Psalm 69, which is one of the most extended imprecatory psalms. How should this psalm shape how we think and feel with God?

The key is going to be how the New Testament authors understand this psalm. We get a lot of help here, because seven of the verses from Psalm 69 are quoted explicitly in the New Testament, including parts that are imprecatory. The New Testament writers did not shy away from imprecatory psalms. In fact, it seems that they found them especially useful in explaining the work of Jesus and what it means for us.

Psalm 69: The Persecuted and His Enemies

The context of Psalm 69 is that David feels overwhelmed by his enemies. These don't seem to be military enemies, but personal enemies, and they are heartless and vicious.

David doesn't claim to be perfect. In fact, he admits in verse 5 that he has committed wrongs and that God knows it: "O God, you know my folly; the wrongs I have done are not hidden from you." But the hostilities against him are not owing to those wrongs: David's enemies hate him *without cause*. They attack him with lies. Verse 4: "More in number than the hairs of my head are those who hate me without cause; mighty are those who would destroy me, those who attack me with lies. What I did not steal must I now restore?"

Zeal for God's Glory

What is at stake in this psalm is that David is jealous for God's glory, and his adversaries reproach him for it. Verse 7: "It is *for your sake* [O God] that I have borne reproach, that dishonor has covered my face." Verse 9: "*Zeal for your house* [O God] has consumed me, and the reproaches of those who reproach you have fallen on me." In other words, his suffering is not only undeserved, but it is endured precisely as a representative of God. "The reproaches of those who reproach you have fallen on me." When God gets reproach, the psalmist gets reproach. The people who hate God also make life hard for David, because he represents God.

Pleading for Rescue

David pleads for God to rescue him from this miserable situation. Verse 14: "Deliver me from sinking in the mire; let me be delivered from my enemies and from the deep waters." Verse 18: "Draw near to my soul, redeem me; ransom me because of my enemies!"

Then come verses 22–28, which are entirely imprecations or curses on his enemies. David prays to God that these enemies—his enemies and God's enemies—will experience the full force of God's judgment and will not be acquitted. David is not praying for their salvation; he's praying for their damnation:

> Let their own table before them become a snare;
> and when they are at peace, let it become a trap.
> Let their eyes be darkened, so that they cannot see,
> and make their loins tremble continually.
> Pour out your indignation upon them,
> and let your burning anger overtake them.
> (vv. 22–24)

Crying for Help

David closes the psalm with another cry for help and a promise of praise. Verses 29–30: "But I am afflicted and in pain; let your salvation, O God, set me on high! I will praise the name of God with a song; I will magnify him with thanksgiving."

In summary, here we have King David—not a perfect man (v. 5), but a righteous man (v. 28), a man who loves the glory of God, who trusts God's mercy for ransom and redemption (v. 18) and who stands up for the cause of the humble (vv. 32–33)—and he is suffering the undeserved persecution of his enemies and God's enemies. In the middle of this lament and cry for help, he devotes seven verses to calling on God to punish these enemies.

Psalm 69 in the New Testament

So how does the New Testament deal with this psalm?

Most importantly, in quoting from this psalm, the New Testament is never embarrassed by it or critical of it. It never treats the psalm as something we should reject or leave behind; it never treats the psalm as *sinful* personal vengeance. We learn from the New Testament, just as we would expect—since Jesus regards the Psalms as inspired by God (Mark 12:36; John 10:35; 13:18)—that this psalm is revered and honored as sacred truth.

The New Testament honors Psalm 69 by quoting from it in at least two important ways: it quotes the psalm as the words of David, and it quotes the psalm as the words of Jesus. Let's take these in turn, and then close this chapter by asking how we ought to read the psalm today and how we should think and feel about David's prayer for the punishment of violent and evil men.

Psalm 69 as the Words of David

First, Romans 11:9–11 quotes Psalm 69:22–23. Here's what the psalm says, "Let their own table before them become a snare; and when they are at peace, let it become a trap. Let their eyes be darkened, so that they cannot see, and make their loins tremble continually."

This is the beginning of David's prayer that God

would pour out his indignation upon his adversaries (v. 24). He prays that just as they gave him poison for food (v. 21), so their table would be their undoing. The very bounty that they think they have would prove to be their judgment. And he prays that they would be blinded and unable to find their way, and that trembling would seize them forever.

In other words, this prayer is a prayer for their condemnation, their destruction, and their damnation. Verses 27–28: "May they have no acquittal from you. Let them be blotted out of the book of the living; let them not be enrolled among the righteous." David consigns them to perdition, to hell.

Not Sinful Personal Vengeance

Now, you would think that if this were sinful personal vengeance, the apostle Paul would at least avoid it and perhaps correct it. But he does just the opposite. He goes straight to this text to support his teaching in Romans 11. He is not the least put off by this psalm. In Romans 11, he teaches that most of Israel has rejected Jesus as her Messiah and has come under God's judgment. The judgment is that a hardening has come on the greater part of Israel so that they will not believe.

Romans 11:7 says: "What then? Israel failed to obtain what it was seeking. The elect obtained it, but the rest were hardened." Paul continues, later in the chapter: "Lest you be wise in your own sight, I do not want you to be unaware of this mystery, brothers: a partial hardening has come upon Israel, until the fullness of the Gentiles has come in" (Romans 11:25). So one of the main teachings of Paul in Romans 11 is that God is judging Israel with this hardening until God's full appointed number of the Gentiles are saved.

Speaking on God's Behalf

In that context, Paul reaches back to the imprecatory Psalm 69 to support his point, quoting verses 22–23 in Romans 11:9–11: "And David says, 'Let their table become a snare and a trap, a stumbling block and a retribution for them; let their eyes be darkened so that they cannot see, and bend their backs forever.'"

In other words, Paul interprets the words of David, not as sinful personal vengeance, but as a reliable expression of what happens to the adversaries of God's anointed. David is God's anointed king, and he is being rejected and reproached and reviled. David manifests a lot of patience in his life (Psalm 109:4), but there comes a point when he speaks as God's inspired, anointed one and, by his prayer, consigns his adversaries to darkness and hardness. They will experience this judgment because David is speaking on God's behalf.

Paul does not hear merely emotional words of retaliation in David's voice. He hears sober, prophetic words of judgment that God's anointed wills to bring on his adversaries. That is why Paul quotes these words in Romans 11, where he is making this very point: the adversaries of Christ, the Messiah of God, are going to be darkened and hardened as part of God's judgment.

The first way the New Testament quotes Psalm 69, therefore, is as prophetic words of judgment by God's inspired spokesman on the adversaries of God's anointed.

Psalm 69 as the Words of Jesus

The second way that the New Testament quotes Psalm 69 is as the words of Jesus himself. The reason for this is that Jesus is the Son of David (Romans 1:3; Matthew

21:15; 22:42) and what happened to David as God's royal anointed one is a foreshadowing of the final Anointed One, the Messiah, Jesus. Jesus read this psalm and saw his own mission being lived out in advance.

Here are four examples of how the New Testament portrays language from Psalm 69 as the words of Jesus.

Jesus Cleansing the Temple

In John 2:13–17, we read about how Jesus drove the sellers out of the temple. Verse 16 says, "And he told those who sold the pigeons, 'Take these things away; do not make my Father's house a house of trade.'" The Bible-saturated disciples see this passion for God's house, and they hear Jesus call the temple "my Father's house," and they remember the words of Psalm 69:9. John 2:17 says: "His disciples remembered that it was written, 'Zeal for your house will consume me.'" Those are the words of Psalm 69:9—which means that the disciples see in David's words and actions a foreshadowing of Christ's words and actions in cleansing the temple.

Jesus Hated by His Own

In John 15:24–25, Jesus is hated by the Jewish leaders in the same way that David was hated by his own people (v. 8). This time, Jesus himself is the one who explicitly quotes Psalm 69 as part of God's "law" or God's instruction. He says, "If I had not done among them the works that no one else did, they would not be guilty of sin, but now they have seen and hated both me and my Father. But the word that is written in their Law must be fulfilled: 'They hated me without a cause.'" This is a quote from Psalm 69:4: "More in number than the hairs of my head are those who hate me without cause."

Jesus himself is aware of David's experience and sees it as foreshadowing his own. Jesus essentially says, "When David is hated by his adversaries, this points to my experience and must be fulfilled in me."

Jesus on the Cross

On the cross, at the most important moment in history, Jesus brings his life to a close by explicitly and overtly fulfilling Psalm 69. In Psalm 69:21 David said, "They gave me poison for food, and for my thirst they gave me sour wine to drink." Evidently Jesus had lived in this psalm and absorbed this psalm and made it part of his very being. Otherwise, I don't know how we could explain John 19:28–30. Here he was, hanging on the cross in horrible agony, and we read:

> After this, Jesus, knowing that all was now
> finished, said (to fulfill the Scripture), "I thirst."
> A jar full of sour wine stood there, so they put a
> sponge full of the sour wine on a hyssop branch
> and held it to his mouth. When Jesus had
> received the sour wine, he said, "It is finished,"
> and he bowed his head and gave up his spirit.

According to the apostle John, Jesus died fulfilling Psalm 69. What more glorious tribute could be paid to a psalm? The very psalm that we tend to think is a problem because of its imprecations was the one Jesus lived in and the one that carried him to the cross and through the cross.

Jesus Enduring Reproach

One more illustration of Psalm 69 as the words of Jesus comes from Romans 15, where Paul is calling Christians to be patient with the weak and to deny themselves and humbly receive others. Amazingly at this point, he reaches back again to Psalm 69:9 and says, "Let each of us please his neighbor for his good, to build him up. For Christ did not please himself, but as it is written, 'The reproaches of those who reproached you fell on me'" (Romans 15:3). Paul takes the words of David and sees them fulfilled in Christ. And the specific thing he focuses on is that Christ endured the reproaches of men willingly.

So it seems that Psalm 69 has two prongs in the New Testament. One prong is judgment: the imprecations are not sinful personal retaliation but prophetic approval of God's just retribution for sin. The other prong is the suffering of God's Anointed One. This suffering is endured for God's sake. And the suffering is either the means by which the adversaries are brought to repentance and saved, or the means by which they are confirmed in their hardness and condemned.

How Should Psalm 69 Affect Us?

We can step back now and ask: How shall we think and feel when we read Psalm 69 today? I'd like to offer three answers to that question.

Approval of God's Judgment

We should hear the divinely inspired voice of David, the Lord's anointed, suffering for the glory of God and expressing his desire for and approval of God's judgment on the unrepentant adversaries of the Lord. David is making plain that God's judgment does come, that it is right and even desirable, and that it should come when the adversaries are beyond repentance. There is a divine judgment coming, and at that day Christians will approve what God does. That is what David's imprecations make plain. That's one thing we should think and feel.

Foreshadowing the Ministry of Jesus

Second, we should recognize that David's experience in Psalm 69 is a foreshadowing of the ministry of Jesus. What David experiences in that psalm as the Lord's anointed, Jesus will experience, and bring to completion, in greater ways in his own suffering and death. The suffering of Jesus will be both a saving suffering and a condemning suffering. For those who accept it as their glory, it will save. For those who are hardened by it, it will condemn.

> Or do you presume on the riches of his kindness and forbearance and patience, not knowing that God's kindness is meant to lead you to repentance? But because of your hard and impenitent heart you are storing up wrath for yourself on the day of wrath when God's righteous judgment will be revealed (Romans 2:4–5).

Incentive to Forgive

Finally, what about us? When we read the words of Psalm 69, what should we personally think and feel and do?

Most importantly, let us not take these words as a license to curse our enemies. In fact, in Paul's mind the psalm takes us in the exact opposite direction. Paul quotes the psalm in Romans 15:3 to encourage us to deny ourselves *rather than* gratify the lust for revenge. "Christ did not please himself, but as it is written, 'The reproaches of those who reproached you fell on me.'" In other words, forbear and forgive.

We want to exercise forgiveness and mercy—but not because there is no wrath, no punishment, or no judgment in Psalm 69. It is precisely because there *is* judgment—judgment which it is not our business to execute. The fact that God will do it, and that it is right for him to do it, is the very means by which we are able to follow Jesus in suffering for the sake of others who have wronged us:

> Beloved, never avenge yourselves, but leave it to the wrath of God, for it is written, "Vengeance is mine, I will repay, says the Lord." To the contrary, "if your enemy is hungry, feed him; if he is thirsty, give him something to drink; for by so doing you will heap burning coals on his head." (Romans 12:19–20)

The burning coals signify penitence and purification where there is repentance, and punishment where there is not. Nobody gets away with anything in this universe. All wrongs will be duly punished, either on the cross of Christ for those who repent, or in hell for those who don't. "Vengeance is mine… says the Lord." God will decide, and we will approve. But until that day of judgment, we follow the words of the Anointed King: "Love your enemies, do good to those who hate you, bless those who curse you, pray for those who abuse you…. You will be sons of the Most High" (Luke 6:27–29, 35).

PSALM 96

Oh sing to the Lord a new song;
sing to the Lord, all the earth!
Sing to the Lord, bless his name;
tell of his salvation from day to day.
Declare his glory among the nations,
his marvelous works among all the peoples!
For great is the Lord, and greatly to be praised;
he is to be feared above all gods.
For all the gods of the peoples are worthless idols,
but the Lord made the heavens.
Splendor and majesty are before him;
strength and beauty are in his sanctuary.

Ascribe to the Lord, O families of the peoples,
ascribe to the Lord glory and strength!
Ascribe to the Lord the glory due his name;
bring an offering, and come into his courts!
Worship the Lord in the splendor of holiness;
tremble before him, all the earth!

Say among the nations, "The Lord reigns!
Yes, the world is established; it shall never be moved;
he will judge the peoples with equity."

Let the heavens be glad, and let the earth rejoice;
let the sea roar, and all that fills it;
let the field exult, and everything in it!
Then shall all the trees of the forest sing for joy
before the Lord, for he comes,
for he comes to judge the earth.
He will judge the world in righteousness,
and the peoples in his faithfulness.

6

Declare His Glory among the Nations

PSALM 96

We have seen that the Psalms are God's words, and that the Psalms are songs, and therefore they aim to *shape our thinking and our feeling*. In chapter one, we looked at Psalm 42 to examine spiritual depression and *how to be discouraged well*. Chapter two was a review of Psalm 51, specifically *how to be brokenhearted well* by guilt and regret. In chapter three, coming out of that discouragement and regret, Psalm 103 taught us the essential importance, especially for parents, of continually expressing *gratitude and praise and blessing* to the Lord. And in chapter four, we learned from Psalm 69 *how to rightly endure opposition, mistreatment, and injustice*.

Now that we know how to process depression and discouragement, how to handle the brokenheartedness of guilt and regret, how to respond to opposition, and how to bless God at all times and in all ways, what could be missing? Where do the Psalms finally take us?

The key and goal of the Psalms, at every point, is Jesus Christ, exalted among all the peoples. No portion of the Psalms—no portion of Scripture—is complete without him, and neither is this book. That is why, in this final chapter, we join the author of Psalm 96 in extolling and glorifying God as sovereign Creator, Savior, and Judge. For the Psalms ultimately take us to the ends of the earth, with a song on our lips, until the day our Savior returns and receives his kingship among all nations.

Music and Missions for the Glory of God

Singing and nations—music and missions—for the glory of God: these are what stand out to me from Psalm 96. How shall we think and feel with God about the nations and about singing and about the glory of the coming king? How are they related in this psalm and in the age to come? And how are they related to Jesus?

God did not make known his ways or reveal his glory or display his marvelous works for you alone, or for your ethnic group alone. He did it with a view to the nations—all the nations. This passage is not referring to political states, but nations, what the psalm calls "peoples," be they Korean or Kurdish, Somali or Sioux, Irish or Italian. Trace with me the focus on the nations in this psalm. The psalmist says that God's people should do at least three things for the nations: *declare* God's glory, *summon* them to join in, and *warn* them of judgment should they fail to do so.

Declare God's Glory

First, we should declare to the nations the truth about God's glory and works and salvation. Verses 2–3: "Sing to the Lord, bless his name; tell of his salvation from day to day. Declare his glory among the nations, his marvelous works among all the peoples!" Tell of his salvation, declare his glory, declare his marvelous works. Do this "among the nations." Do this "among *all* the peoples." All of them. Leave none out. And then, in keeping with verse 10, sum up your declaration with the message of the kingship of God over the nations. "Say among the nations, 'The Lord reigns!'"

Summon the Nations to Join In

Second, we should summon the nations to join us, the people of God, in ascribing glory to him and singing praise to him. Verse 7: "Ascribe to the Lord, O families of the peoples, ascribe to the Lord glory and strength!" Verse 1: "Sing to the Lord, all the earth!" Don't just tell the earth facts about the greatness and the glory of God—bid them to join you in praising him. Call for their conversion. All the nations must bow before the one true God of Israel, whom we know now as the Father of our Lord Jesus the Messiah.

Warn Them of Judgment

Third, let's not merely declare God's glory to the nations, or merely summon them to join us in ascribing glory to him. Let us also warn them of the reason for this declaration and summons: because they are depending on false gods and judgment is coming on all the nations. Verse 5: "All the gods of the peoples are worthless idols, but the LORD made the heavens." Verse 10: "Yes, the world is established; it shall never be moved; he will judge the peoples with equity." Verse 13: "He comes, for he comes to judge the earth. He will judge the world in righteousness, and the peoples in his faithfulness."

In other words, when the psalmist says, "sing to the LORD, *all* the earth" (v. 1), and "declare… his marvelous works among *all* the peoples" (v. 3), and "he is to be feared above *all* gods" (v. 4), and "tremble before him, *all* the earth" (v. 9), and "*all* the gods of the peoples are worthless idols" (v. 5), he really means all! The God of the Psalms lays claim on the allegiance of every people—all of them, in all their unimaginable diversity of culture and religion.

Missions: Glorious Call to the Nations

Do not, the psalm implies, leave out any nation, any people, or any family—all of them must convert to the true and living God and abandon all their other gods. Do not let any unloving trend of multiculturalism make you shrink back from the loving work of calling every people from every other religion to repent and ascribe all glory to the one and only true and living God.

Consider this passage from the New Testament, in which I have replaced "Gentiles" with the equivalent term "nations":

> "I will praise you among the [nations], and sing to your name." And again it is said, "Rejoice, O [nations], with his people." And again, "Praise

> the Lord, all you [nations], and let all the
> peoples extol him." And again Isaiah says, "The
> root of Jesse will come, even he who arises to
> rule the [nations]; in him will the [nations]
> hope." (Romans 15:9–12)

These quotes are from the Psalms, Deuteronomy, and
Isaiah. Paul the apostle piles them up, one after another, to
support the coming of Jesus as the Messiah *for all nations.*
That's especially clear from the two preceding verses: "I
tell you that Christ became a servant to the circumcised
[the Jews] to show God's truthfulness, in order to confirm
the promises given to the patriarchs, and in order that the
Gentiles [the nations] might glorify God for his mercy. As
it is written,..." (Romans 15:8–9). Then come the Old Testament promises summoning all the nations to praise God
for his mercy—for the work of Jesus Christ on the cross
in dying for sinners, thus making mercy possible for rebel,
Gentile sinners like us.

How should you and I feel about this emphasis,
across the Old and New Testaments, on all the nations and
all the peoples? God is not telling us this so that we feel
exhausted, but rather that we feel exhilarated! And this
encouragement is for both missionary *goers* and missionary *senders*—all of us who believe in the one true God,
revealed most fully in the God-man, Jesus Christ.

Why do I say this? Look at verse 1 of Psalm 96, where
the missionary impulse to all the nations flows *from*
singing and calls *for* singing: "Oh sing to the LORD a new
song; sing to the LORD, all the earth!" This is a singing
mission, an exhilarating mission. This is the way you feel
when your team has won the cross-town rivalry or the

Super Bowl or the World Cup—only a thousand times greater. "Declare his glory among the nations, his marvelous works among all the peoples!" (v. 3). We are speaking of *glory*. We are speaking of marvelous works, not boring works or ordinary works. We have tasted and seen that this God is greater to know than all other greatness. "Great is the LORD, and greatly to be praised" (v. 4). We are thrilled and exhilarated to know him and sing to him, and we summon the world—*all* the peoples—to sing with us to him.

Largest Cause of All

If you are one who can say from the heart, "Jesus is Lord," then you were made for this. When you confess Jesus as the Lord of the universe, you sign up for significance beyond all your dreams. Whether you're a businessman, a homemaker, or a student, to belong to Jesus means that you must embrace the nations for which he died and over which he will rule. Your heart was made for this, and until you embrace this global calling there will always be a measure of sickness in your soul—a partial emptiness where God's passion for his glory among the nations belongs.

In the early 1900s, the Laymen's Missionary Movement was born among businessmen who were captured by a holy ambition to get behind what God was doing in the massive Student Volunteer Movement. Here is what J. Campbell White, the first secretary of the Laymen's Missionary Movement, said:

> Most men are not satisfied with the permanent output of their lives. Nothing can wholly satisfy the life of Christ within his followers except the

adoption of Christ's purpose toward the world he came to redeem. Fame, pleasure, and riches are but husks and ashes in contrast with the boundless and abiding joy of working with God for the fulfillment of his eternal plans. The men who are putting everything into Christ's undertaking are getting out of life its sweetest and most priceless rewards.[6]

How should you feel about the global purpose of Jesus Christ to be glorified among all the nations? You should feel like this cause is the consummation of your significance in life. Many other things are important, but this is the largest cause of all. Every consistent follower of the Lord of Lords and King of Kings embraces this purpose. Every healthy Christian finds the consummation of his existence in being a part of this great purpose—that God be glorified among all the nations.

Condition of the Cause

What is the situation among the nations today? Stunning shifts are taking place as God gathers his elect *from* all the nations and sends his church *to* all the nations—indeed from everywhere to everywhere. Europe and America are no longer the center of gravity in world Christianity. The center is shifting south and east. Latin America, Africa, and Asia are experiencing phenomenal growth and are becoming the great sending churches.[7]

Organizations such as Joshua Project and People Groups are showing us who the "nations" actually are—how many such groups there are and how reached or unreached with the gospel they are. As of this writing,

Joshua Project says that there are 7,840 "unreached" or "minimally reached" people groups (both categories are defined in part as having fewer than 2 percent evangelicals). Together, these two groups compose a shocking 45.3 percent of the world population.

I thank God that there are people doing this difficult research to help us understand the task that remains before us. Go to these websites, and start learning about the global situation. And then dream about how your life, whether as goer or sender, might be more fully involved in declaring God's glory among the nations—his marvelous works among all the peoples.

How should you feel about the nations of the world? You should have a passion for their salvation. You should be thrilled that God rules over them all and calls us to be his emissaries to them all, with the best news in the world. You should be exhilarated that God will have a people of his own from all the nations, singing to him and ascribing glory and strength to his Son.

You were made for this kind of joy. All the other joys of the Psalms, all the other emotions of the Psalms, are taking us here: the glory of God celebrated and sung by all the peoples of the earth.

Music: Striking the Singing Note

As we have already glimpsed, flying like a banner over all the emphasis on the nations in Psalm 96 are verses 1 and 2, and they are all about singing. "Oh sing to the LORD a new song; sing to the LORD, all the earth! Sing to the LORD, bless his name; tell of his salvation from day to day." Why would you begin such a psalm—about the global reach of God's kingdom and the duty to "tell of his salvation from day to day" (v. 2) and to "declare his glory among the nations" (v. 3)—with the command to sing to the Lord?

The answer is simple: you can't summon the nations to sing if *you* are not singing. And we *are* summoning the nations—all the nations—to sing to the Savior and Judge of all the earth. Our goal is not mere belief or mere behavior changes. Our goal is whole-hearted, whole-minded, whole-souled joy in God that overflows in song. "Let the nations be glad and sing for joy" (Psalm 67:4).

New Song in Our Day

But why *new* songs? Notice that these new songs are *to* the Lord and not just *about* the Lord. "Oh sing *to the* LORD a new song; sing *to the* LORD, all the earth!" (v. 1). It's not wrong to sing about the Lord. The Psalms do it all the time. But when new songs are being written and sung "to the Lord," something is happening in the church. It's a sign of unusual life and vibrancy. People are not just living off the spiritual capital of previous generations, but they are dealing vibrantly with the living God and their songs are being sung *to* him. He is real. He is personal. He is known. He is precious. He is present. And when these songs are beautiful and biblical and engaging, worship is often more intense and more personal.

That is what the psalm calls for, and that is what has been happening during my entire adult life. Around the world there is a new song and a new vibrancy and a new personal engagement in singing to the Lord. And the astonishing thing in our time is the way this awakening of singing to the Lord with new songs has such a strong global and missionary flavor.

To my knowledge, singing has never been more at the forefront of missions than it is today. God is doing something wonderful in the fulfillment of Psalm 96. It is far bigger than any one denomination, any one mission, any one ethnic group, or any one region of the world. The global church is singing—singing to the Lord, singing new songs, and singing about God's Lordship over the nations.

Center of Our Singing

Psalm 96 is calling us to spread a passion for the glory of God in all things for the joy of all peoples. And it is calling us to summon these peoples to ascribe glory to God through song. This is both the hardest and the happiest business in the world. So in concluding this book, I would simply say: don't miss what God is doing. Be a part of it. Get the nations on your heart. Think rightly about God's global purposes. Feel deeply about his marvelous works. Sing with all your heart to the Lord. Be a part of summoning the nations to join you. And may the center of our singing be the same as the center of the new song we will sing in the age to come, namely, the song of the Lamb who was slain.

> And they sang a new song, saying, "Worthy are you to take the scroll and to open its seals, for you were slain, and by your blood you ransomed people for God from every tribe and language and people and nation, and you have made them a kingdom and priests to our God, and they shall reign on the earth." (Revelation 5:9–10)

A Closing
Invitation

Try to imagine the Bible without the Psalms. What a different book it would be! What a different place the church would be. And what a different person I would be.

It's not as though the rest of the Bible does not teach truth and awaken emotions. I learn things and feel things everywhere I read in the Bible. But it's not the same. The Psalms do not just awaken the affections of the heart; they put the expression of those affections in the foreground. They feature the emotional experience of the Psalmist intentionally against the backdrop of divine truth.

They do not just invite the emotion of the heart in response to revealed truth. They put the emotion on display. They are not just commanding; they are contagious. We are not just listening to profound ideas and expressed affections. We are living among them in their overflow. We are walking in the counsel of God-besotted wisdom, and standing in the way of amazed holiness, and sitting in the seat of jubilant admiration.

We touch pillows wet with tears. We hear and feel the unabashed cries of affliction and shame and regret and grief and anger and discouragement and turmoil. But what makes all this stunningly different from the sorrows of the world is that all of it—absolutely all of it—is experienced in relation to the totally sovereign God.

None of these emotions rises from a heart that has rejected the all-governing God. "*Your* waves have gone over me" (Psalm 42:7). "*You* have made my days a few hand-breadths" (Psalm 39:5). "*You* have rejected us and disgraced us and have not gone out with our armies" (Psalm 44:9). "*You* have made us like sheep for slaughter and have scattered us among the nations" (Psalm 44:11). "*You* have made your people see hard things" (Psalm 60:3). And in it all, "O LORD, *you* have searched me and known me!" (Psalm 139:1). God is behind everything.

This is the great difference between the Psalms of Scripture and the laments, complaints, and sorrows of the world. For the psalmists, God is a rock-solid, unshakeable, undeniable, omnipotent Reality. Their emotional experiences get their meaning not by denying him or his power or his wisdom, but by dealing with him as he is—absolutely sovereign. "Whatever the LORD pleases, he does, in heaven and on earth, in the seas and all deeps" (Psalm 135:6). This was the psalmists' unshakeable conviction—all of them: "Our God is in the heavens; he does all that he pleases" (Psalm 115:3).

They never turned against God and rejected him because of their calamities. The fool says in his heart that there is no God (Psalm 14:1), but not the psalmist. It was unthinkable to the psalmists that their sorrows should drive them away from God. Where would they go? "If I ascend to heaven, you are there! If I make my bed in Sheol, you are there!" (Psalm 139:8). If God is God, then all emotional life is lived in his presence. He makes sense of it. Or there is no sense.

But sheer omnipotence is not the main reason that the psalmists never forsake their God. The psalmists know from experience that he is good and faithful. They know that, if they trust him, he will act on their behalf (Psalm 37:5). They testify of this again and again.

> You have multiplied, O Lord my God, your wondrous deeds and your thoughts toward us. (Psalm 40:5)

> You have drawn me up and have not let my foes rejoice over me. (Psalm 30:1)

> You have given me the shield of your salvation. (Psalm 18:35)

> You have given me relief when I was in distress. (Psalm 4:1).

> You have healed me. (Psalm 30:2)

> You have been the helper of the fatherless. (Psalm 10:14)

> You have maintained my just cause. (Psalm 9:4)

> You have turned for me my mourning into dancing. (Psalm 30:11)

> You have put more joy in my heart than they

have when their grain and wine abound. (Psalm 4:7)

In great mercy and wisdom God has chosen to give us the Psalms. He has put them at the very center of Scripture. Surely this is no accident. The heart is the center of our emotional life. And God's heart-book is at the center of the Bible. How easy it is to find! This is an invitation. God wants our hearts. He will take them as he finds them. And then, with the healing contagion of the Psalms, he will shape them.

Accept his invitation to come. On the front door, he has promised, *Enter here. Find your delight in lingering here in meditation.* You will be "like a tree planted by streams of water that yields its fruit in its season, and its leaf does not wither. In all that he does, he prospers" (Psalm 1:3).

Author

John Piper is a founder of desiringGod.org, and chancellor of Bethlehem College & Seminary in Minneapolis, Minnesota. He served for 33 years as pastor of Bethlehem Baptist Church and is author of more than 50 books. More than 30 years of his sermons and articles are available at desiringGod.org.

Endnotes

1. "It is significant that the Psalter also consists of five books (Psalms 1–41, 42–72, 43–89, 90–106, and 107–150). The editors of the Psalter wanted readers to grasp the analogy between the Torah, God's "instruction" par excellence, and the Psalter. In short, the Psalter is to be read and heard as God's instruction to the faithful. Regardless of the fact that the Psalms originated as the response of faithful persons to God, they are now to be understood also as God's Word to the faithful." J. Clinton McCann, *A Theological Introduction to the Book of Psalms: The Psalms as Torah* (Nashville: Abingdon Press, 1993), 27.
2. "The Psalms can and should be part of the constant practice of the presence of God. Regularly read from beginning to end, they lead us again and again to consider aspects of life and of God's will that we might not otherwise choose to remember or confront—let alone to embody in our living. Memorized in chunks, the Psalms can provide ready responses to the pressing realities of our days. When I have wakened in a panic in the darkness of the early morning hours—submerged in fear, self-pity, or self-doubt—the Psalms have often provided the assurance that my anxieties are known by God, who enlightens my dark places. So, I encourage you to make the Psalms your constant companion. Keep a copy at hand, and keep their words in your mind and heart and on your lips as you meet the challenges of your days and nights." Gerald Wilson, *The NIV Application Commentary, Psalms Vol. 1* (Grand Rapids: Zondervan, 2002), 104.
3. It seems plausible to me that the psalmist has recorded his responses in a way that can appear somewhat backward to us, recording his most recent response at the start of the psalm.
4. Martyn Lloyd-Jones, *Spiritual Depression*, (Grand Rapids: Eerdmans, 1965), pp. 20–21.
5. Jonathan Edwards, *Religious Affections* (New Haven: Yale University Press, 1959), pp. 339f.
6. J. Campbell White, "The Laymen's Missionary Movement," in *Perspectives on the World Christian Movement*, ed. Ralph D. Winter and Steven C. Hawthorne (Pasadena, Calif." William Carey Library, 1981), 225.
7. See, for example, Philip Jenkins's books *The Next Christendom and The New Faces of Christianity*.

desiringGod

Everyone wants to be happy. Our website was born and built for happiness. We want people everywhere to understand and embrace the truth that God is most glorified in us when we are most satisfied in him. We've collected more than thirty years of John Piper's speaking and writing, including translations into more than forty languages. We also provide a daily stream of new written, audio, and video resources to help you find truth, purpose, and satisfaction that never end. And it's all available free of charge, thanks to the generosity of people who've been blessed by the ministry.

If you want more resources for true happiness, or if you want to learn more about our work at Desiring God, we invite you to visit us at www.desiringGod.org.

---

www.desiringGod.org

Made in the USA
Lexington, KY
08 December 2017